50 Fruit Smoothie Recipes

(50 Fruit Smoothie Recipes - Volume 1)

Carie Brown

Content

50 Awesome Fruit Smoothie Recipes

***

1. Aaron's Energy Fruit Smoothie

Serving: 3 serving(s) | Prep: 3mins | Ready in:

Ingredients

- 1 1/2 cups frozen whole strawberries
- 1 cup frozen mango
- 1/2 cup non-fat vanilla yogurt
- 1 cup fresh banana (a whole banana)
- 3/4 cup pomegranate-blueberry juice
- 1 1/2 cups diet V8 splash (Berry Blend)
- 1/4 cup nutritional yeast flakes
- 3 tablespoons Splenda granular

Direction

- In a blender, puree all ingredients on low, to get the ball rolling.
- After 5 seconds or so, crank it to high and puree for another 10 seconds.

Nutrition Information

- Calories: 153.5
- Total Fat: 1.1
- Sodium: 11.1
- Fiber: 7.2
- Sugar: 17.6
- Saturated Fat: 0.2
- Total Carbohydrate: 33.7
- Cholesterol: 0
- Protein: 7.3

2. Anything Goes Fruit Smoothie

Serving: 2-4 serving(s) | Prep: 5mins | Ready in:

Ingredients

- 1 (20 ounce) can crushed pineapple with juice
- 1 cup plain nonfat yogurt
- 1 banana, cut into chunks
- 1 cup pineapple juice
- 1/2 cup strawberries or 1/2 cup raspberries (or black berries, blueberries, etc...i've never tried it with these however)
- 1/2 cup ice cube

Direction

- Blend all ingredients in a blender until smooth.
- ENJOY!
- (How much simpler is that?!?!?).

Nutrition Information

- Calories: 369
- Sodium: 101.2
- Fiber: 4.8
- Protein: 9.5
- Total Fat: 0.9
- Saturated Fat: 0.2
- Sugar: 71.7
- Total Carbohydrate: 86.2
- Cholesterol: 2.5

3. Anything Goes Fruit And Nut Smoothie

Serving: 2 serving(s) | Prep: 5mins | Ready in:

Ingredients

- 3 tablespoons nut butter, your choice

- 1 cup non-dairy milk substitute (I always use vanilla soymilk)
- 1 banana, frozen
- 1 cup frozen fruit, your choice
- 1 tablespoon maple syrup
- 1 tablespoon flax seed oil

Direction

- In a blender or food processor, blend all ingredients until smooth.
- If you like a thinner shake, add more milk.

Nutrition Information

- Calories: 138.7
- Total Fat: 7
- Sodium: 1.5
- Sugar: 13.2
- Protein: 0.6
- Saturated Fat: 0.7
- Fiber: 1.5
- Total Carbohydrate: 20.2
- Cholesterol: 0

4. Banana Date Smoothie

Serving: 12 ounces, 2 serving(s) | Prep: 10mins | Ready in:

Ingredients

- 1 cup low-fat plain yogurt
- 1/2 cup skim milk, 1% is fine too
- 1/2 cup dates, fresh, pitted and chopped
- 2 bananas, sliced
- 8 ice cubes

Direction

- Place everything in blender and blend until the ice cubes are well incorporated.
- Serve in two chilled glasses.
- How easy is that :).

Nutrition Information

- Calories: 311.1
- Fiber: 6
- Cholesterol: 8.6
- Total Fat: 2.6
- Sodium: 126.5
- Sugar: 46.3
- Total Carbohydrate: 66.6
- Protein: 11.1
- Saturated Fat: 1.5

5. Banana And Ginger Wake Up Call Smoothie

Serving: 3 serving(s) | Prep: 10mins | Ready in:

Ingredients

- 1 peach, halved and pitted
- 6 strawberries
- 1/2 banana, cut into chunks
- 1/2 teaspoon fresh gingerroot, finely chopped
- 2/3 cup evaporated milk
- 1 teaspoon vanilla extract
- 4 -6 ice cubes
- ground cinnamon, to decorate

Direction

- Place the fruits and ginger in a blender with the milk and vanilla extract.
- Blitz together, adding one ice cube at a time.
- Pour into glasses, sprinkle with cinnamon and serve.

Nutrition Information

- Calories: 117.3
- Protein: 4.5
- Total Fat: 4.5
- Saturated Fat: 2.6
- Sodium: 60.6
- Total Carbohydrate: 15.3

- Fiber: 1.5
- Sugar: 6.5
- Cholesterol: 16.2

6. Banana And Oat Smoothie

Serving: 1 serving(s) | Prep: 5mins | Ready in:

Ingredients

- 2 small bananas (or 1 large banana)
- 7 fluid ounces ice cold milk
- 1 tablespoon rolled porridge oats
- 2 ice cubes

Direction

- Place all ingredients into the blender, mix for approximately 30 seconds.

Nutrition Information

- Calories: 335.2
- Protein: 9.9
- Saturated Fat: 5.1
- Fiber: 5.8
- Total Carbohydrate: 59.4
- Sugar: 24.8
- Cholesterol: 29.9
- Total Fat: 8.8
- Sodium: 108.2

7. Banana, Peach And Passionfruit Smoothie

Serving: 2 serving(s) | Prep: 5mins | Ready in:

Ingredients

- 1 cup skim milk
- 200 g low-fat sugar-free peach mango yogurt
- 2 small bananas

- 1 tablespoon honey
- 2 passion fruit
- 1 dash nutmeg

Direction

- Combine the milk, yoghurt, banana and honey and passion fruit in a blender. Blend until smooth and thick.
- Pour into a long serving glass and sprinkle with nutmeg.

Nutrition Information

- Calories: 190
- Sodium: 79
- Sugar: 23
- Total Carbohydrate: 42.8
- Cholesterol: 2.5
- Protein: 6.4
- Total Fat: 0.8
- Saturated Fat: 0.3
- Fiber: 4.5

8. Blackberry And Apple Smoothie

Serving: 1 serving(s) | Prep: 7mins | Ready in:

Ingredients

- 3⁄4 cup blackberry
- 1⁄4 cup unsweetened applesauce
- 1⁄4 cup plain fat-free yogurt
- 1 cup skim milk
- 1 mint leaf, for garnish

Direction

- Reserve three blackberries and put remainder into a blender or food processor. Add applesauce, yogurt and milk. Blend or process for 15 to 20 seconds until smooth.
- Pour into a glass and decorate with reserved blackberries and mint.

Nutrition Information

- Calories: 207.9
- Total Carbohydrate: 35.6
- Cholesterol: 6.2
- Saturated Fat: 0.5
- Sugar: 10
- Sodium: 194.6
- Fiber: 6.5
- Protein: 14.9
- Total Fat: 1.3

9. Breakfast Fruit Smoothie

Serving: 1 serving(s) | Prep: 5mins | Ready in:

Ingredients

- 1 cup pineapple
- 1 cup ice
- 1/2 cup blueberries
- 1/2 cup raspberries
- 1/2 cup low-fat vanilla yogurt

Direction

- Throw in blender.
- Blend until smooth.

Nutrition Information

- Calories: 251.8
- Fiber: 7.9
- Cholesterol: 6.1
- Total Fat: 2.4
- Saturated Fat: 1
- Sodium: 88.5
- Sugar: 41.2
- Total Carbohydrate: 54.3
- Protein: 8.2

10. Cherry And Papaya Smoothie

Serving: 2 serving(s) | Prep: 5mins | Ready in:

Ingredients

- 1 1/2 cups white grape juice
- 1 tablespoon honey
- 2 cups bing cherries, stemmed, pitted
- 1 cup papaya, peeled, diced
- 1 large banana, frozen

Direction

- Put all ingredients in a blender process until smooth.
- Pour into two tall glasses ENJOY!

Nutrition Information

- Calories: 607.3
- Total Fat: 1.4
- Sugar: 137.5
- Protein: 4.2
- Cholesterol: 0
- Saturated Fat: 0.4
- Sodium: 22
- Fiber: 6.9
- Total Carbohydrate: 152.5

11. Chocolate Smoothie W/ Blueberries And Pineapple

Serving: 1-2 serving(s) | Prep: 3mins | Ready in:

Ingredients

- 1/4 cup coffee creamer
- 1 3/4 cups milk
- 1/2 cup frozen blueberries
- 1 cup of frozen pineapple
- 2 tablespoons cocoa powder
- 1 tablespoon sugar

Direction

- (Feel free to add ice to thicken)
- Blend till well mixed.

Nutrition Information

- Calories: 639.3
- Total Fat: 29
- Sodium: 238.4
- Fiber: 8.4
- Total Carbohydrate: 87.8
- Cholesterol: 99.4
- Saturated Fat: 17.8
- Sugar: 51.8
- Protein: 19.1

12. Cinnamon Roasted Apples

Serving: 8 apple halves, 4-8 serving(s) | Prep: 10mins | Ready in:

Ingredients

- 1/4 cup packed light-brown sugar
- 2 tablespoons fresh lemon juice
- 4 gala apples or 4 fuji apples
- 4 cinnamon sticks, plus more for garnish

Direction

- Preheat oven to 450.
- In a large bowl, combine sugar, lemon juice, and 1/4 cup water.
- Halve apples and core using a spoon or melon baller. Toss apples in the sugar.
- Arrange apples, skin up in a baking dish then pour sugar over them. Tuck in cinnamon sticks and cover with foil.
- Bake until apples are easily pierced about 15-20 minutes.

Nutrition Information

- Calories: 148.5
- Saturated Fat: 0.1

- Fiber: 4.4
- Cholesterol: 0
- Protein: 0.5
- Total Fat: 0.3
- Sodium: 5.7
- Sugar: 32.4
- Total Carbohydrate: 39.1

13. Coffee Bananas Foster Smoothie

Serving: 2 serving(s) | Prep: 5mins | Ready in:

Ingredients

- 1 1/2 cups strong brewed coffee, chilled
- 1/2 teaspoon ground cinnamon
- 2 tablespoons dark brown sugar
- 2 small ripe bananas
- 6 ounces cups vanilla yogurt
- 1/2 cup fat-free half-and-half
- 1 cup ice cube

Direction

- Combine all ingredients in a blender container.
- Process until very smooth and frothy.
- Pour into two glasses and serve.

Nutrition Information

- Calories: 233.9
- Fiber: 3
- Sugar: 32.8
- Total Fat: 4
- Saturated Fat: 2.4
- Sodium: 139.2
- Total Carbohydrate: 46.6
- Cholesterol: 14.2
- Protein: 5.9

14. Date With A Melon Smoothie

Serving: 2 serving(s) | Prep: 5mins | Ready in:

Ingredients

- 10 pitted dates, diced
- 2/3 cup boiling water
- 1 1/2 cups peach nectar
- 1 tablespoon honey
- 2 cups cantaloupe, diced
- 2 large bananas

Direction

- In a container, combine dates boiling water, then set aside for 15 minutes before covering chilling in the refrigerator for 2 hours.
- When chilled, drain the dates, then in a blender, combine the dates all the other ingredients, processing until smooth.
- Pour into 2 tall glasses ENJOY!

Nutrition Information

- Calories: 425.2
- Saturated Fat: 0.2
- Total Carbohydrate: 109.9
- Cholesterol: 0
- Protein: 4.4
- Total Fat: 0.9
- Sodium: 42.9
- Fiber: 9.4
- Sugar: 64.1

15. Dole's Berry Fruit Smoothie 100% Dv Of Vitamin C

Serving: 4 Smoothies, 4 serving(s) | Prep: 10mins | Ready in:

Ingredients

- 20 ounces crushed pineapple, drained
- 2 bananas (small, ripe, peeled)
- 2 cups frozen strawberries, sliced
- 1 pint vanilla frozen yogurt
- 1 tablespoon flax seed (optional)
- 1 tablespoon wheat germ (optional)
- 1 tablespoon vanilla protein powder (optional)
- 2 tablespoons vanilla-flavored soymilk (optional)

Direction

- Slice bananas into blender or food processor container.
- Add pineapple and strawberries.
- Cover; blend until smooth.
- Add yogurt; blend until thick and creamy.
- Enjoy!

Nutrition Information

- Calories: 293.6
- Sodium: 66.9
- Sugar: 50
- Cholesterol: 1.4
- Protein: 4.6
- Total Fat: 4.5
- Saturated Fat: 2.5
- Fiber: 5
- Total Carbohydrate: 63.2

16. Easy, Healthy Fruit Smoothie!

Serving: 4 medium-sized cups full, 4 serving(s) | Prep: 2mins | Ready in:

Ingredients

- 1 3/4-2 cups milk
- 1 cup banana, frozen
- 1 cup blueberries, frozen
- 1 cup strawberry, frozen
- 1/2 cup raspberries, frozen
- ice, if using fresh fruit (desired amount)
- honey (for taste) (optional) or Agave (for taste) (optional)

Direction

- Put all ingredients in blender, except Agave or honey. Set blender on "ice crush" setting and blend until mixed.
- Pour into cups, and add desired amount of honey or agave until sweetened.

Nutrition Information

- Calories: 141.9
- Total Carbohydrate: 23.4
- Sodium: 53.6
- Fiber: 3.6
- Sugar: 10.6
- Cholesterol: 14.9
- Protein: 4.6
- Total Fat: 4.4
- Saturated Fat: 2.5

17. Fresh Fruit Smoothies

Serving: 2-4 serving(s) | Prep: 5mins | Ready in:

Ingredients

- 2 cups fresh strawberries
- 2 large bananas
- 1 1/2 cups cranberry juice
- 5 ice cubes
- 2 teaspoons honey

Direction

- Clean the strawberries and remove the stems.
- Peel the bananas and break it into chunks.
- Place the strawberries and the bananas into a blender.
- Then add the fruit juice, ice cubes, and the honey.
- Place the lid on the blender.
- Fold a kitchen towel over the blender so that it drapes over the top.
- Turn the blender on high and blend the shake until smooth.

- Always keep your hand over the lid so that it doesn't come off.

Nutrition Information

- Calories: 290.6
- Sodium: 8.5
- Fiber: 6.4
- Sugar: 51.9
- Total Carbohydrate: 73.5
- Protein: 2.5
- Total Fat: 1.1
- Saturated Fat: 0.2
- Cholesterol: 0

18. Frosty Fruit Smoothies

Serving: 2 serving(s) | Prep: 2mins | Ready in:

Ingredients

- 1 cup orange juice, chilled
- 1/2 cup nonfat milk
- 1 medium banana, cut into chunks
- 1 teaspoon vanilla
- 1/2 cup small ice cubes or 1/2 cup crushed ice

Direction

- In a blender, combine fruit juice and milk; add banana and vanilla.
- Add ice cubes, Cover and blend until nearly smooth.

Nutrition Information

- Calories: 135.8
- Saturated Fat: 0.2
- Sodium: 34.5
- Cholesterol: 1.2
- Protein: 3.6
- Total Carbohydrate: 29.6
- Total Fat: 0.6
- Fiber: 1.8

- Sugar: 21

19. Frozen Fruit Smoothie

Serving: 1 serving(s) | Prep: 5mins | Ready in:

Ingredients

- 1/2 cup frozen strawberries
- 1/2 cup frozen blueberries
- 1/2 cup cottage cheese or 1/2 cup yogurt
- 1/4 cup milk
- 1/3 cup orange juice

Direction

- Place ingredients in blender.
- Mix until smooth.
- Enjoy!

Nutrition Information

- Calories: 310.9
- Fiber: 5
- Sugar: 37.5
- Protein: 15.2
- Total Fat: 7.2
- Saturated Fat: 3.2
- Sodium: 416.3
- Total Carbohydrate: 50.3
- Cholesterol: 26.4

20. Fruit Carrot Smoothie

Serving: 2-4 serving(s) | Prep: 10mins | Ready in:

Ingredients

- 2 apples, quartered
- 1 banana, cut into fourths
- 1/2 cup plain fat-free yogurt
- 1/4 cup powdered soy protein concentrate

- 1/4 cup ground flax seed
- 1/2 teaspoon sugar substitute (I use Stevia)
- 1 1/2 cups frozen strawberries
- 3/4 cup ice cube
- 2 carrots, chunked
- 1/2-1 cup pineapple juice
- 1/2-1 cup water (or more juice)

Direction

- Place all ingredients into blender in the order listed. Run on high for approximately 2 minutes (I use a Vita-mix).
- Enjoy a really healthy lunch or breakfast smoothie!

Nutrition Information

- Calories: 352.7
- Sodium: 102.1
- Sugar: 43.8
- Cholesterol: 1.2
- Total Fat: 6.8
- Saturated Fat: 0.7
- Total Carbohydrate: 71.1
- Protein: 8.6
- Fiber: 14

21. Fruit Smoothie Ice Cream

Serving: 2 serving(s) | Prep: 10mins | Ready in:

Ingredients

- 2 over-ripe bananas
- 1 small apple
- 1/2 teaspoon vanilla
- 1/8 teaspoon cinnamon
- 1/8 teaspoon nutmeg

Direction

- Peel, core, and chop up apple.
- Put in microwave safe dish and cook until softened.

- Mash apple and let cool.
- Mash 2 bananas with apple.
- Add vanilla and spices.
- Stir well and put in 1/2 cup portion dishes.
- Cover with Saran Wrap and freeze.

Nutrition Information

- Calories: 136.7
- Fiber: 4.5
- Sugar: 20.1
- Protein: 1.4
- Total Fat: 0.5
- Saturated Fat: 0.2
- Sodium: 1.9
- Total Carbohydrate: 34.6
- Cholesterol: 0

22. Fruit And Veggie Smoothie

Serving: 4 cups, 4 serving(s) | Prep: 10mins | Ready in:

Ingredients

- 1 cup apple juice
- 1 cup sliced apple (use sweet apples)
- 1/4 cup applesauce
- 1/2 cup carrot, sliced
- 1/2 cup cucumber, peeled and sliced
- 2 cups ice
- 1 teaspoon ground cinnamon

Direction

- Blend the apples with veggies until smooth. Add ice and ground cinnamon and serve cold.

Nutrition Information

- Calories: 64.6
- Total Fat: 0.2
- Sodium: 18.9
- Fiber: 1.7
- Protein: 0.4

- Saturated Fat: 0
- Sugar: 10.5
- Total Carbohydrate: 16.5
- Cholesterol: 0

23. Garden Fruit Smoothie

Serving: 16 fluid ounces, 1 serving(s) | Prep: 6mins | Ready in:

Ingredients

- 1/2 cup grapes
- 1/2 cup blueberries
- 1/2 banana
- 1/2 apple
- 2 teaspoons ground flax seeds
- 1/4 teaspoon ground cinnamon
- 1 ounce fresh spinach (rinsed well)
- 2 teaspoons minced ginger (frozen works very well)
- 1/2 cup water

Direction

- Place all ingredients in blender container and process until smooth. Adjust consistency by adding more water if desired.
- Serve immediately, or refrigerate up to 6 hours.

Nutrition Information

- Calories: 232.8
- Saturated Fat: 0.4
- Sodium: 34.1
- Cholesterol: 0
- Fiber: 8.7
- Sugar: 36
- Total Carbohydrate: 54.2
- Protein: 3.9
- Total Fat: 3

Serving: 1-2 serving(s) | Prep: 3mins | Ready in:

Ingredients

- 2 kiwi fruits, peeled
- 25 green grapes, frozen
- 1 green apple, sliced
- 4 -5 ice cubes
- orange juice or apple juice, to smooth it out

Direction

- Blend all ingredients until smooth.

Nutrition Information

- Calories: 2352.3
- Total Fat: 6.1
- Sodium: 71.5
- Fiber: 36.9
- Sugar: 518.9
- Protein: 24.7
- Saturated Fat: 1.8
- Total Carbohydrate: 615.5
- Cholesterol: 0

┌───┐
│ **25. Healthy Blackberry And Banana**   │
│ **Smoothie**   │
└───┘

Serving: 2 serving(s) | Prep: 5mins | Ready in:

Ingredients

- 4 ice cubes (about 1/4 of a cup)
- 1 1/4 cups frozen blackberries
- 1/2 cup skim milk
- 1 medium banana, broken into about 1 inch chunks
- 1 -6 ounce dannon light and fit reduced-fat blackberry yogurt or 1 -6 ounce other similar artifically sweetened yogurt

- artificial sweetener, packets (optional)

Direction

- Place ice cubes in bottom of blender, followed by the rest of the ingredients. Puree on high about 1 minute, or until all ingredients are incorporated together. Pour into two tall glasses. Serve immediately.

Nutrition Information

- Calories: 153
- Sodium: 47.9
- Saturated Fat: 0.3
- Fiber: 6.2
- Sugar: 17.3
- Total Carbohydrate: 34.3
- Cholesterol: 2.1
- Protein: 4.9
- Total Fat: 0.9

┌─────────────────────────────────┐
│ **26. Island Fruit Smoothie**   │
└─────────────────────────────────┘

Serving: 1 serving(s) | Prep: 5mins | Ready in:

Ingredients

- 1 small banana, peeled and cut into chunks
- 2 tablespoons coconut milk
- 2 tablespoons lime juice
- 1/4 cup orange juice
- 1/4 cup pineapple juice
- 1/2 teaspoon ginger, grated
- 3 ice cubes

Direction

- Put all ingredients in blender until smooth.

Nutrition Information

- Calories: 220.6
- Total Fat: 7

- Sugar: 24.3
- Cholesterol: 0
- Saturated Fat: 5.8
- Sodium: 9.6
- Fiber: 3.1
- Total Carbohydrate: 41.6
- Protein: 2.6

27. Kate's Healthy Fruit Smoothie

Serving: 8 oz., 2 serving(s) | Prep: 5mins | Ready in:

Ingredients

- 1/2 banana, frozen
- 1/2 cup strawberry, frozen
- 1 cup skim milk
- 1/2 cup oatmeal
- 1 tablespoon flax seed, whole
- 1 tablespoon bee pollen
- 1 tablespoon wheat germ
- 2 probiotic capsules

Direction

- Blend flax seed and oatmeal until well blended.
- Add fruit, milk the remainder of the ingredients blend well.
- Divide into 2 glasses and enjoy!

Nutrition Information

- Calories: 206.4
- Total Fat: 4.3
- Saturated Fat: 0.7
- Sodium: 76
- Fiber: 5.3
- Sugar: 5.7
- Total Carbohydrate: 33.3
- Cholesterol: 2.5
- Protein: 10.4

28. Low Fat Fruit Smoothie

Serving: 2-4 serving(s) | Prep: 5mins | Ready in:

Ingredients

- 1 cup low-fat plain kefir
- 1 banana
- 1 cup frozen strawberries
- 3/4 cup frozen blueberries
- 1 1/2 cups frozen sliced peaches
- 2 (1 g) packets Splenda sugar substitute
- 1/4 cup vanilla-flavored soymilk (optional)

Direction

- Pour the Kefir into a blender.
- Add the banana and blend.
- Add the other fruits and Splenda.
- Blend, on a lower speed at first, but finish off with the higher speed (like frappe).
- If the smoothie seems too thick (sometimes the fruit is juicier than other times) add the Vanilla Soymilk.
- Pour into glasses and serve while it is still cold.
- Rinse out your blender and the glasses as soon as they are emptied for easier clean-up.

Nutrition Information

- Calories: 340.6
- Total Fat: 0.7
- Saturated Fat: 0.1
- Sodium: 14.9
- Fiber: 9.1
- Sugar: 71.7
- Cholesterol: 0
- Total Carbohydrate: 88.4
- Protein: 2.6

Serving: 2-4 serving(s) | Prep: 20mins | Ready in:

Ingredients

- 1 mango, peeled,stoned and chopped
- 1 pink grapefruit, peeled and as much pith removed as possible
- 1 peach, peeled,stoned and chopped
- 14 ounces low fat fromage frais or 10 ounces natural yoghurt or 7 ounces cold milk

Direction

- Purée all of the ingredients together in a liquidizer/blender until smooth, then chill.

Nutrition Information

- Calories: 181.7
- Total Fat: 1
- Sugar: 37.7
- Protein: 3
- Saturated Fat: 0.2
- Sodium: 1.7
- Fiber: 5.8
- Total Carbohydrate: 45.4
- Cholesterol: 0

30. Meal Replacement Fruit Smoothies

Serving: 1 serving(s) | Prep: 5mins | Ready in:

Ingredients

- 1 cup skim milk or 1 cup soymilk or 1 cup milk or 1 cup fruit juice, of your choice
- 1 3/4 cups sugar-free fat-free frozen yogurt, flavor of your choice
- 1 cup frozen fruit, such as berries,pineapple,banana,etc.,cut large fruit into chunks before freezing (Drained canned fruit works very well)
- 1/4 cup Splenda sugar substitute (optional)
- 1 packet carnation instant breakfast drink mix (from a 6.3 oz. box. Your choice of flavors)

Direction

- Pour milk or fruit juice into smoothie maker or blender (ALWAYS add all liquid ingredients to smoothie maker or blender FIRST).
- Add instant breakfast powder and Splenda, if using, to smoothie maker or blender.
- Add frozen yogurt to milk mixture.
- Add fruit to smoothie mixture.
- Place top on blender or top and stir stick on smoothie maker and blend well.
- Note: Larger chunks of fruit will not be as easy to measure, either measure them out before freezing and store in single-serving containers or use twice the amount of frozen fruit in blender or smoothie maker.
- If mixture is too thick when blended add a little more milk or fruit juice until desired consistency.
- Pour and enjoy!

Nutrition Information

- Calories: 100.9
- Cholesterol: 4.9
- Total Carbohydrate: 13.7
- Sodium: 145.1
- Fiber: 0
- Sugar: 0
- Protein: 9.7
- Total Fat: 0.6
- Saturated Fat: 0.4

31. Megan's Fruit Smoothies

Serving: 4 serving(s) | Prep: 5mins | Ready in:

Ingredients

- 8 ounces strawberry yogurt

- 1 cup orange juice
- 3 ounces raspberry Jell-O gelatin (uncooked or as a powder)
- 8 -10 large strawberries
- 10 ice cubes

Direction

- Mix together in a blender until you get your desired consistency.

Nutrition Information

- Calories: 179.9
- Total Fat: 1
- Saturated Fat: 0.5
- Sodium: 137.9
- Sugar: 25.2
- Cholesterol: 3.4
- Protein: 5.1
- Fiber: 0.8
- Total Carbohydrate: 39

32. Mixed Fruit Smoothie

Serving: 2 serving(s) | Prep: 3mins | Ready in:

Ingredients

- 1/2 cup of fresh strawberry
- 1 chopped apple (Remove the skin.)
- 1 chopped banana
- 1 cup milk
- ice cream or yogurt (preferable)

Direction

- Blend these ingredients together to make a zesty yet creamy smoothie, banana and strawberry blend really well whilst the apple gives the smoothie a bit of zest, I find this to be a very filling smoothie.

Nutrition Information

- Calories: 178
- Saturated Fat: 2.9
- Sugar: 16.1
- Total Carbohydrate: 31.4
- Total Fat: 4.9
- Sodium: 61.4
- Fiber: 3.9
- Cholesterol: 17.1
- Protein: 5.1

33. Mixed Fruit And Spinach Smoothie

Serving: 1 serving(s) | Prep: 5mins | Ready in:

Ingredients

- 1/2 banana
- 1/3-1/2 cup frozen blueberries
- 1/3-1/2 cup frozen blackberrie
- 1/4-1/2 cup frozen spinach, large pieces broken up
- 1/2 cup pineapple chunks in juice (tidbits or crushed pineapple would work just as well, if not better)

Direction

- Throw everything in the blender and puree until smooth. You might need to add additional pineapple juice or a tiny bit of water if you like to use a straw! I usually use a spoon to eat mine.

Nutrition Information

- Calories: 233.5
- Total Fat: 0.9
- Sugar: 46
- Total Carbohydrate: 59.4
- Protein: 3.6
- Saturated Fat: 0.2
- Sodium: 32
- Fiber: 7.9

- Cholesterol: 0

34. Oatmeal Fruit Smoothie

Serving: 1 serving(s) | Prep: 1mins | Ready in:

Ingredients

- 1/2 cup steel cut oats
- 1/2 cup frozen fruit
- 1/2 cup ice cube
- 1 g stevia
- ground cinnamon, to taste
- 1 cup water

Direction

- Pulse oats in blender until powdery.
- Add 1 cup of water and incorporate the other ingredients.
- Blend until smooth.

Nutrition Information

- Calories: 303.4
- Sugar: 0
- Total Carbohydrate: 51.7
- Cholesterol: 0
- Protein: 13.2
- Sodium: 12.2
- Fiber: 8.3
- Total Fat: 5.4
- Saturated Fat: 0.9

35. Pumpkin Fruit Smoothie

Serving: 1 large smoothie, 1 serving(s) | Prep: 5mins | Ready in:

Ingredients

- 1/2 cup pumpkin puree
- 1 banana, frozen and broken into chunks
- 1/3 cup applesauce (I had yummy homemade stuff!)
- 1/3 cup orange juice (I used clementine juice)
- 2 tablespoons cream of coconut
- 1/2 teaspoon pumpkin pie spice
- 1/4 cup water
- sugar (optional) or your choice artificial sweetener, if desired (optional)

Direction

- Place ingredients in a food processor, blender or a large jug if using an immersion blender (got to love 'em!).
- Blend till completely smooth. Taste, adjust flavors if necessary. Serve with a warm slice of peanut butter toast for a filling, delicious breakfast. :-).

Nutrition Information

- Calories: 297.7
- Total Fat: 7.6
- Saturated Fat: 6.2
- Fiber: 5.5
- Sugar: 24.6
- Protein: 3.7
- Sodium: 47
- Total Carbohydrate: 60
- Cholesterol: 0

36. Quick 'n Easy Strawberry And Banana Smoothie

Serving: 3-4 serving(s) | Prep: 5mins | Ready in:

Ingredients

- 250 g strawberries, hulled
- 1 medium banana, peeled and roughly chopped
- 300 ml 1% low-fat milk
- 150 ml natural yoghurt

- 15 ml spoon clear honey

Direction

- Place all the above ingredients into a blender and blend until smooth.
- Adjust the sweetness according to taste and pour into serving glasses.

Nutrition Information

- Calories: 137.8
- Saturated Fat: 1.1
- Sodium: 55
- Total Carbohydrate: 27.2
- Cholesterol: 7.6
- Protein: 5.1
- Total Fat: 2
- Fiber: 2.7
- Sugar: 20.9

37. Single Serving Fruit Smoothie

Serving: 1 1/2 cups, 1 serving(s) | Prep: 5mins | Ready in:

Ingredients

- 1⁄4 cup skim milk
- 6 ounces fat free sugar free yogurt
- 1⁄4 cup water
- 1⁄2 cup frozen raspberries
- 1 tablespoon oatmeal

Direction

- Using a 2 cup measuring glass, add milk and yogurt, then add frozen fruit.
- Add oatmeal and water.
- Use immersion blender to blend ingredients.
- If you do not have an immersion blender, you can use a regular blender.
- If you like a thicker smoothie, so not use the water.

Nutrition Information

- Calories: 173
- Protein: 4.1
- Fiber: 6
- Total Carbohydrate: 39.4
- Cholesterol: 1.2
- Sodium: 38.9
- Sugar: 27.3
- Total Fat: 0.7
- Saturated Fat: 0.2

38. Soy Fruit Smoothie

Serving: 1-3 serving(s) | Prep: 5mins | Ready in:

Ingredients

- 1⁄2 cup blueberries
- 1⁄2 cup cranberries
- 1⁄2 cup strawberry
- 1⁄4 cup of purple grapes
- 1 banana
- 1 cup vanilla-flavored soymilk

Direction

- Make sure to rinse all fruit before putting them in the blender!
- I suggest using all FRESH fruits, frozen fruits can lose nutritional values.
- Put all ingredients in a blender
- Here you can add certain things, for example, I add 2 TBSP's of benefiber, and a TBSP of essential greens powder, and 2 TBSP of an amino acid complex.
- But that is COMPLETELY optional.
- Once all the ingredients are in, turn the blender on, and let it run for a good minute to make sure everything is mixed up.
- After the process is done you can drink one shake, and save the other for later on, drink them both, save them both, whatever you want!

- Just remember that the fridge life is 4 days, to maintain the best taste, and optimal nutritional values.
- ENJOY!

Nutrition Information

- Calories: 218.8
- Protein: 2.8
- Total Fat: 1
- Sodium: 4.4
- Total Carbohydrate: 56
- Saturated Fat: 0.2
- Fiber: 8.8
- Sugar: 33.1
- Cholesterol: 0

39. Spinach, Pear And Peach Smoothie....don't Knock It Till You Try

Serving: 8 oz, 1 serving(s) | Prep: 1mins | Ready in:

Ingredients

- 1 cup baby spinach leaves, raw
- 1/2 cup frozen sliced peaches
- 1/2 cup fresh pear, diced
- 1/2 cup water

Direction

- Tear spinach leaves and put in blender.
- Dice pear and put in blender
- Put frozen peaches in blender
- Add water and blend of about a minute.

Nutrition Information

- Calories: 172.2
- Total Fat: 0.4
- Sugar: 35.9
- Protein: 2

- Saturated Fat: 0
- Sodium: 34.4
- Fiber: 5.5
- Total Carbohydrate: 43.8
- Cholesterol: 0

40. Strawberry Banana Fruit Smoothie

Serving: 1 serving(s) | Prep: 5mins | Ready in:

Ingredients

- 2 cups frozen unsweetened strawberries
- 1/4 cup unsweetened frozen blueberries
- 1/2 banana
- 3/4 cup unsweetened frozen sliced peaches
- 1 cup skim milk
- 1/2 cup light strawberry yogurt

Direction

- Put the milk in your blender first, then the yogurt. Then add blueberries, peaches, banana and half of the strawberries last. Blend then add the other half of strawberries. I do it this way because some blenders have a real hard time blending frozen strawberries and doing it this way may help. Pour in a tall glass (it makes A LOT) grab a straw and enjoy.

Nutrition Information

- Calories: 327.8
- Total Fat: 1.5
- Sodium: 155
- Protein: 12.4
- Saturated Fat: 0.5
- Fiber: 11.9
- Sugar: 30.6
- Total Carbohydrate: 72.2
- Cholesterol: 4.9

41. Strawberry And Watermelon Smoothies

Serving: 4 serving(s) | Prep: 5mins | Ready in:

Ingredients

- 12 strawberries, hulled
- 1 ounce fresh mint leaves
- 1 seedless watermelon

Direction

- Place the strawberries in a blender and add the mint. Whizz to blend.
- Add the watermelon pulp to the blender and whizz again. Serve immediately.

Nutrition Information

- Calories: 355.4
- Sodium: 13.9
- Sugar: 71.7
- Total Carbohydrate: 89.1
- Protein: 7.4
- Total Fat: 1.9
- Saturated Fat: 0.2
- Fiber: 5.8
- Cholesterol: 0

42. Summer Fruit Smoothie

Serving: 4 , 4 serving(s) | Prep: 5mins | Ready in:

Ingredients

- 2 (16 ounce) cans apricots or 2 (16 ounce) cans peaches or 2 (16 ounce) cans pears or 2 (16 ounce) cans pineapple or 2 (16 ounce) cans fruit cocktail, in any combination packed in juice
- 2 tablespoons fresh lemon juice
- 1 pint frozen yogurt or 1 pint fruit sherbet

Direction

- Drain fruit, reserving 1 cup of the juice. Purée fruit with reserved juice and lemon juice in a blender. Add frozen yogurt in small chunks, blending just until smooth. Serve immediately in tall glasses with straws.
- Nutritional Information Per Serving: Calories 210; Total fat 3g; Saturated fat 2g; Cholesterol 10mg; Sodium 65mg; Carbohydrate 46g; Fiber 3g; Protein 4g; Vitamin A 20%DV*; Vitamin C 20%DV; Calcium 10%DV; Iron 6%DV.
- *Daily Value.

Nutrition Information

- Calories: 185.7
- Protein: 7.5
- Saturated Fat: 2.6
- Sodium: 58.3
- Fiber: 4.6
- Sugar: 27
- Cholesterol: 15.8
- Total Fat: 4.8
- Total Carbohydrate: 31.7

43. Summer Fruits Smoothie

Serving: 7 1/2 pint Servings | Prep: 8mins | Ready in:

Ingredients

- 500 g frozen summer fruit
- 450 g virtually plain fat-free yogurt
- 700 ml uht skim milk
- 3 teaspoons Splenda granular, artificial sweetener
- 2 medium bananas

Direction

- Cut up the bananas and put into blender with half the yogurt, half milk and sweetener then blitz it till bananas are broken down.

- Put in about half the berries (frozen) slowly, while it's blending.
- Add the rest of the yogurt and milk to loosen up the mixture.
- Add the rest of the berries, blend till completely mixed.

Nutrition Information

- Calories: 106.3
- Cholesterol: 3.2
- Protein: 8
- Total Carbohydrate: 18.1
- Sodium: 107.9
- Fiber: 0.9
- Sugar: 9.1
- Total Fat: 0.5
- Saturated Fat: 0.3

44. Three Fruit Smoothie

Serving: 3 | Prep: 5mins | Ready in:

Ingredients

- 2 bananas
- 4 peaches, sliced
- 8 strawberries
- 2 -3 cups apple juice (depending on how thick you want it)
- 1/4 teaspoon cinnamon

Direction

- Combine ingredients. Blend in blender until smooth. Pour into glasses and enjoy!
- You may garnish with a strawberry, if desired.

Nutrition Information

- Calories: 209.4
- Total Carbohydrate: 52.4
- Protein: 2.4
- Total Fat: 0.9

- Sugar: 40.1
- Sodium: 6.1
- Fiber: 4.9
- Cholesterol: 0
- Saturated Fat: 0.1

45. Tropical Fruit Smoothie...mmm

Serving: 3-4 serving(s) | Prep: 10mins | Ready in:

Ingredients

- 1 (14 ounce) can coconut milk
- 1 (20 ounce) can pineapple chunks in juice
- 1 ripe mango
- 1 tablespoon brown sugar (optional)

Direction

- Chill can of coconut milk in the fridge.
- Open can of pineapple and place two to three chunks of pineapple into each square of ice cube tray, pour remaining juice into tray over the chunks. Freeze until solid.
- Peel mango and chop into pineapple chunk sized cubes and freeze in a ziplock bag or plastic freezer container.
- Once fruits are frozen, pulse in food processor or blender until you have small, fine bits. I use six pineapple cubes and 1/4 of the mango per serving.
- Add coconut milk until desired consistency and add brown sugar.
- Leave leftover fruits in freezer for next time and leave coconut milk in a sealed jar in the fridge for future use.
- I have also added one frozen banana to the mix and/or a handful of frozen strawberries.

Nutrition Information

- Calories: 423.5
- Total Carbohydrate: 52.9
- Protein: 4.9

- Fiber: 5.8
- Saturated Fat: 21.8
- Sodium: 72.3
- Sugar: 46
- Cholesterol: 0
- Total Fat: 24.8

46. Tropical Fruit Smoothie

Serving: 2 serving(s) | Prep: 5mins | Ready in:

Ingredients

- 1⁄2 small papaya
- 1⁄2 pear
- 1⁄2 nectarines or 1⁄2 peach
- 1⁄2 banana
- 1 (6 ounce) container yogurt (I like to use pineapple flavor)

Direction

- Whirl everything together and enjoy!
- If the mixture is thick, you can always add a little milk or juice, or add an orange to the combo to lighten it up a bit.

Nutrition Information

- Calories: 132.4
- Total Fat: 3.1
- Sodium: 41.3
- Sugar: 16.6
- Total Carbohydrate: 24.5
- Saturated Fat: 1.9
- Fiber: 3.3
- Cholesterol: 11.1
- Protein: 4

47. Vanilla Fruit Smoothies

Serving: 2 large smoothies | Prep: 2mins | Ready in:

Ingredients

- 1⁄2 cup orange juice
- 1⁄2 cup plain low-fat yogurt
- 1 ripe banana
- 1⁄3 cup frozen peaches
- 1⁄3 cup frozen strawberries
- 1⁄4 cup frozen raspberries
- 1 teaspoon vanilla extract
- 8 ice cubes

Direction

- Put all ingredients in a blender and blend the heck out of it. If the blender can't handle ice, then crush the ice before blending.
- Drink.
- YUMMY!

Nutrition Information

- Calories: 209.2
- Total Carbohydrate: 46
- Cholesterol: 3.7
- Sodium: 49.5
- Fiber: 4.5
- Sugar: 34.7
- Total Fat: 1.4
- Saturated Fat: 0.7
- Protein: 4.9

48. Vegetables, Fruits And Flax Smoothie

Serving: 6 serving(s) | Prep: 10mins | Ready in:

Ingredients

- 2 tablespoons ground flax seeds
- 1 mango
- 1 green apple
- 1 banana
- 1 cup fresh kale (organic, chopped)
- 1 cup fresh spinach (organic, chopped)

- 2 medium carrots
- 1 celery rib
- 5 cups water
- 1/2 teaspoon honey (optional)
- 8 ice cubes

Direction

- Lightly roast and grind the flax seeds.
- Rinse all vegetables.
- Peel and chop the carrots, apple, mango and banana.
- Mix all ingredients and blend in the food processor. Serve it immediately.
- Serving 6 Persons.
- P.S. Roasting the flax seeds not required. But make sure that the flax seeds are crisp dry.

Nutrition Information

- Calories: 95.5
- Sodium: 36.6
- Fiber: 3.8
- Total Fat: 1.5
- Saturated Fat: 0.2
- Protein: 1.9
- Sugar: 14.3
- Total Carbohydrate: 21.2
- Cholesterol: 0

49. Yummu Fruit Smoothie

Serving: 1 serving(s) | Prep: 10mins | Ready in:

Ingredients

- 1 ripe banana
- 4 frozen strawberries
- 1 (6 ounce) container plain fat-free yogurt (any flavor)
- 3 -5 ice cubes
- 1/4 cup 1% low-fat milk

Direction

- Toss all the ingredients into a blender and mix for about two minutes.
- You can also substitute any of the fruits for anything else you might like!

Nutrition Information

- Calories: 240.4
- Total Fat: 1.3
- Sodium: 160.7
- Cholesterol: 6.4
- Protein: 13.2
- Saturated Fat: 0.7
- Fiber: 4
- Sugar: 32.5
- Total Carbohydrate: 46.9

50. Zucchini, Apple And Banana Smoothie

Serving: 1 serving(s) | Prep: 5mins | Ready in:

Ingredients

- 1 cup zucchini
- 1 large apple, cored
- 1/2 frozen banana
- 1/2 cup water

Direction

- Combine all ingredients in blender.
- Process until smooth.

Nutrition Information

- Calories: 189.6
- Saturated Fat: 0.2
- Sugar: 33.5
- Total Carbohydrate: 48.1
- Protein: 2.7
- Total Fat: 1
- Sodium: 16.3

- Fiber: 8.1
- Cholesterol: 0

Index

Conclusion

Thank you again for downloading this book!

I hope you enjoyed reading about my book!

If you enjoyed this book, please take the time to share your thoughts and post a review on Amazon. It'd be greatly appreciated!

Write me an honest review about the book – I truly value your opinion and thoughts and I will incorporate them into my next book, which is already underway.

Thank you!

If you have any questions, **feel free to contact at:** *author@cookbookgarden.com*

Carie Brown

cookbookgarden.com